The Ultimate US Error Coin Guide

Owen J Steele

If this book inspires even one person, I will have achieved something meaningful.

Preface

This book examines Owen Steele's work, exposing how it deceives collectors into viewing him as a credible figure rather than a profiteer exploiting the uninformed. An anonymous numismatic expert systematically refutes each claim with accurate data. Steele's apparent lack of research or deliberate fabrication of numismatic details raises questions about why his work continues to attract buyers.

The book begins with some credibility but deteriorates as later chapters read like they were written by a child.

I'm frustrated by books like this that spread misinformation and damage the hobby. Collectors, misguided by such work, present coins with inaccurate claims.

Owen Steele

Steele's book is entirely fraudulent, and he's reaping the profits with a smirk. Many of his claims are utterly laughable, paired with numerous inaccurate coin depictions, as demonstrated by the book's flawed content. He is praying on the naive and the uninformed. If you believe Steele's book is a professional handbook, despite its inclusion of randomly selected error coins, some misidentified, you are greatly mistaken.

Writing Skills and Foreign Sources

Most of the non-credible books begin with polished, professional writing, employing sophisticated vocabulary, but gradually shifts to simpler, everyday language. This suggests it may be compiled from multiple sources, revealing a lack of consistent expertise. The language shifts from intellectual and professional to everyday words, often with spelling and grammar mistakes.

Most of the error coin books aren't written by verified numismatists based in the U.S. A review of 150 author names shows 95% have English origins. This suggests many books come from Europe or Asia, using European English for translation. Many of these books give away the origin by selecting words not commonly used in the USA to describe something. Owen Steele's book fits into this scenario with a British name and writing the indicates foreign writing.

Dishonesty Tactics

Some authors use aliases and tweaked titles to dominate market share, often landing multiple books under 100,000 BSR. Fake bios, stolen photos, and fabricated editorials abound. Monthly, new guides appear—amateur efforts with obvious errors, typically languishing above 1 million Best Seller Rank (BSR), lost in obscurity.

Other error coin guides, such as the one published under the name Owen Steele, top the BSR charts with a consistent ranking of around 5,000, translating to approximately 20 to 40 books sold daily. With 73 pages and a sale price of $19.98, the estimated profit is $10 per book, potentially yielding a monthly profit of $6,000 to $12,000. This is significant for a self-published book, despite some credibility concerns. However, caution is warranted: most books fail to sell any copies, and the next closest BSR for a similar book is around 25,000.

Amazon's minimal barriers to self-publishing enable the production of numerous books, often under different pseudonyms, containing identical content. Additionally, Amazon permits plagiarism by allowing individuals to use photos stolen from Heritage Auctions and other sources.

Credible Authors
The books by these authors are accurate and credible. I found no issues with the information, and it seems these authors are numismatists based in the USA.

- Blake Alma (since 2018)
- Sam Sommer (since 2017)
- Kenneth Bressett & Brian Allen (since 2018)
- Stan McDonald (since 2009)
- Justin Couch (since 2023)

Challenge

I'll offer $1,000 to anyone who can find a self-published book on Amazon that is more accurate than those by the credible authors listed above. The book must have an Amazon Best Seller Rank below 75,000 to qualify, as I've read all of them.

Explosion of Error Coin Guides on Amazon

Self-published error coin books have surged. As of May 2025, 203 remain active, a testament to the trend's scale.

	March 2025	May 2025
Row Labels	Books remaining	Books remaining
2002	1	1
2005	1	1
2007	1	1
2010	1	1
2011	0	0
2014	0	0
2016	1	1
2017	4	4
2018	4	4
2019	7	7
2020	9	9
2021	14	14
2022	14	14
2023	28	28
2024	73	73
2025	27	45
Grand Total	185	203

The books listed in the chart represent the remaining books available at a specific point in time, as books are frequently removed or go out of print. Since tracking started in 2024, a total of 121 books were added that year, while 41 books were either removed due to infringement or withdrawn by the author.

New Releases and Market Trends

As of May 20, 2025, forty-three new error coin books surfaced for 2025. The surge likely stems from opportunists exploiting Amazon's lax publishing rules, chasing profit. Yet over 47% of these books fail, with a Best Seller Rank (BSR) above one million signaling zero sales. More than 80% of coin books sell just 0–4 copies daily.

Amazon Book Rank	March 2025 Books	May 2025 Books
Books Over 1,000,000	115	133
500,000 - 999,999	26	25
200,000-499,999	15	15
100,000-199,999	4	10
50,000-99,999	6	9
35,000-49,999	4	2
20,000-34,999	8	4
10,000-19,999	2	3
5,000-9,999	2	1
1-4,999	0	1
C-10	182	203

The threshold is a BSR of 35,000, which corresponds to an average monthly profit of $1,000, the minimum amount this book deems acceptable. Ninety-one percent of books fail to meet this objective on Amazon with most books with no profit.

Most books cap at under 120 pages, minimizing printing costs to boost profit. A 100-page book priced at $14.97 yields about $6.95 per sale.

The worst sources of coin knowledge are self-proclaimed experts who easily publish inaccurate information or steal internet photos. Books advocating coin cleaning or spreading vague, incorrect info mislead new collectors, who deserve accurate guidance to avoid pitfalls.

Not all books have been fully reviewed, so other credible authors may exist. Want a coin book assessed? I'll buy and review it—email fredwright3414@gmail.com.

Best Seller Ranking
Decoding Amazon's BSR and its link to sales is tricky, but a test book offers insights. Authors can choose up to three categories; most coin books target Antique & Collectible Coins & Medals (Books) the sole coin-specific option.

Amazon's BSR algorithm, reset hourly, shifts rankings dynamically, but its mechanics remain opaque. Websites offer conflicting sales estimates per rank, prompting a detailed study later in this book.

Amazon's ranking system is significantly impacted by advertising. When a book is promoted through ads, it is nearly certain to achieve a Best Sellers Rank (BSR) below 60,000. However, the book's actual sales figures might not differ from when its BSR exceeded 100,000. Since advertising distorts the BSR, books that are advertised may not necessarily be among the top sellers.

Original Sources for Numismatics
Confidence in reliable sources has been supplanted by misinformation and faulty data, encompassing 95% of the books on Amazon and most internet sources chasing clicks.

Once, collectors relied on trusted sources like the ANA, reputable magazines, books, and dealers. Pre-internet, experts like Bill Fivaz and J.T. Stanton cataloged 99% of RPM and doubled die errors, John Wexler advanced CONECA's work (still active online), James Wiles documented varieties at Variety Vista, and Kenneth Bressett and Q. David Bowers penned guides since 1946. Stan McDonald has contributed articles and books since
1999. These authorities face baseless attacks today.

How this book will never make you an expert

No books on Amazon that are self-published will make you an expert. Most of the books will make you stupid and the author rich.

There are very few authors that are credible, and their books are designed to provide collectors with information that can be used to better understand error coins.

As previously stated, these are the only trustworthy authors with credible information.
- Blake Alma (since 2018)
- Sam Sommer (since 2017)
- Kenneth Bressett & Brian Allen (since 2018)
- Stan McDonald (since 2009)
- Justin Couch (since 2023)

Chapter One – Owen Steele

Owen Steele's book is not in the norm, since it has somehow reached a milestone in Amazon's Best Seller Rank. Why this book is the bestselling self-published book for error coins is not well understood.

Analyzing the book
This book aligns with a trend among error coin guides on Amazon, frequently using an old English name. Over 90% of these self-published books exhibit this characteristic, raising questions about their origins. It's highly probable that many of these books are authored by foreign writers who adopt an English name for the book.

The author's photo may cast doubt on the book's credibility, yet no one has remarked on the clothing style or the dated background. It could be authentic but is looks suspicious. Although there is no proof this photo is photoshopped, it does not negatively impact the sales of the book.

The book cover is unremarkable, following a trend of featuring an American flag with additional elements. Its colors—mainly gold, black, and white—align with another popular trend. Given that many books share this style, it's unlikely the cover drives the book's popularity.

Analyzing the Summery
All the self-published books have some form of click bait in the summary like promises of finding a rare coin or becoming an expert in coin collecting.

The summary presents some enticing questions. *"Are you tired of wondering if you've missed valuable error coins in your collection?*

"Do you find yourself questioning whether that unusual mark is a genuine mint error or just damage?

"Have you ever dreamed of discovering a rare error variety worth thousands but lack the confidence to identify it?[1]"

The book's stated purpose is to offer methods for identifying valuable error coins in a personal collection, distinguishing them from merely damaged coins. However, it fails to provide guidance on finding rare coins in a collection or distinguishing between damaged coins and genuine error coins.

"Every day, valuable coins pass through countless hands unnoticed. Even experienced collectors sometimes overlook rare varieties worth significant premiums because they lack the specialized knowledge to identify them. But what if you could develop the same keen eye and technical expertise that professional numismatists use to discover and authenticate valuable error coins? This guide transforms you from an uncertain collector into a confident expert!"
With professional authentication techniques and detailed images, this comprehensive handbook provides everything you need to identify, authenticate, and value the most sought-after mint error varieties.[2]"

---

[1] Summary from Owen Steele's book
[2] Summary from Owen Steele's book

Many books overstate the likelihood of finding rare varieties in pocket change, but it's as probable as discovering gold in your backyard. For this guide to claim it can make someone an expert, statements like the 1937-D three-legged Buffalo nickel being a die break error reveal a lack of coin knowledge, making such promises highly doubtful.

"Inside, you'll discover:

✓ Professional detection methods to identify valuable errors others frequently miss
✓ Expert authentication techniques used by leading grading services
✓ Clear images of genuine error varieties for confident identification
✓ Specialized knowledge to distinguish authentic errors from post-mint damage
✓ Step-by-step examination methods for accurate attribution
✓ Insider tips for building a distinguished error collection
✓ Professional preservation techniques to maintain maximum value[3]"

This checklist is handy, but the book offers nothing to help anyone become an expert, as much of its content is inaccurate.

---

[3] Summary from Owen Steele's book

The biography

Owen Steele's passion for error coins began in 1978 when, as a young bank teller, he discovered a 1972 Doubled Die Lincoln Cent in his daily transactions. This find sparked a twenty-five-year journey in professional numismatics, including two decades as an authentication specialist at a leading grading service. A respected lecturer at major coin shows and contributor to numismatic publications, Steele has dedicated his life to helping collectors develop the expert eye needed to spot valuable errors. His systematic approach to error authentication, refined through examining thousands of coins, forms the foundation of this comprehensive guide.

If he was 25 in 1978 while working as a bank teller, he would be 72 in 2025. The author's photo indicates he might be in his 60s or 70s, though this cannot be confirmed.

The book's first fabrication is the assertion that he was an authentication specialist at a leading grading service, a respected lecturer at major coin shows, and a contributor to numismatic publications. No one at PCGS, NGC, or ANACS recognizes his name in any capacity. It's unlikely he was a lecturer, and he certainly did not contribute to numismatic publications.

The exaggerated biography might mislead a novice into believing the author is credible, lending false legitimacy to the book's content. This could be a leading reason people are buying this book.

From the Publisher
Steele tries to persuade readers to purchase his book by showcasing three "distinguished" individuals who allegedly endorse the guide. However, none of these individuals are credible, and their statements cannot be verified as authentic. While some might assume these people were interviewed for a self-published book, this is highly unlikely.

Editorial Reviews
Amazon allows book writers to add editorials. Any book that is self-published with editorials are fabricated. There are no sources that allow people to write editorials for self-published books on Amazon.

★ ★ ★ ★ ★ The New Standard in Error Attribution
Finally, a guide that reveals the actual methods used by professional graders. The detailed imagery and precise attribution points make complex error

identification clear and practical. Worth every penny for serious collectors.
Reviewed by Dr. Gregory S. Whitmore, Numismatic Researcher

★ ★ ★ ★ Professional Expertise Made Accessible

Outstanding combination of professional techniques and practical application. The systematic approach and visual guides give collectors real confidence in identifying valuable errors. A must-have for building a distinguished collection.
Reviewed by Walter R. Sheffield, Professional Numismatist

★ ★ ★ ★ ★ Essential Reference for Authentication

Brilliant blend of expert knowledge and practical guidance. The detailed analysis and extensive visual documentation make error identification straightforward and reliable.
Reviewed by Robert L. Montgomery, Editor, Numismatic Review

★ ★ ★ ★ ★ Expert Methods Revealed

The authentication techniques and detailed images in this guide have completely transformed my error hunting success. Now I spot valuable varieties others miss entirely. Indispensable for

serious collectors.
Reviewed by David S. Winchester, Professional Dealer

★ ★ ★ ★ ★ Error Attribution Mastery

Transforms complex error authentication into clear, actionable knowledge. The visual guides and professional techniques have dramatically improved my detection skills. A must-have reference.
Reviewed by Dr. Victor R. Fairfield, Numismatic Consultant

★ ★ ★ ★ ★ Professional Knowledge Unlocked

This guide delivers exactly what serious collectors need: professional techniques for identifying valuable errors. The detailed images and step-by-step methods have revolutionized my collecting approach.
Reviewed by Marcus A. Thompson, Senior Numismatist

The Book Content Disputes the Author's Expertise

A true numismatist can readily spot inaccuracies and misleading claims by Steele. These errors directly contradict his assertions of being an authenticator or contributing to numismatic organizations.

The book mistakenly attributes the 1937-D three-legged Buffalo nickel to a die break, which is incorrect. Steele's reference to this error should be enough to return the book to Amazon for full credit.

Consider the 1804 dollar, now one of the most famous and valuable U.S. coins. While not an error in the traditional sense, its accidental creation in 1834

The 1804 silver dollar was not minted by mistake. It was deliberately struck in 1834 and subsequent years for special coin sets presented to dignitaries.

You'll know exactly what to look for when examining a 1982 Lincoln cent, potentially uncovering a rare no-brass specimen worth thousands.

Steele does not offer the facts about the 1982 Lincoln cent mintages in the book leaving the reader wondering what brass cent to look for. In 1982, Denver and Philadelphia minted both copper and copper-plated zinc cents, except for one variant: no 1982-D small date copper cents were produced. Seven distinct issues were created that year.

seemingly minor misalignment in the Lincoln Memorial columns on a 1999 Wide AM cent can command a premium. This expertise will

This claim targets novices who might fall for Steele's bold exaggerations. There are no rare 1999 Wide AM cents with misaligned columns, as this isn't feasible since dies are created from pre-designed hubs. However, the 1999 Lincoln cent with a "Wide AM" is a valuable variety because a proof die was mistakenly used to mint some circulation coins.

treasures to be preserved. Mint employees were often penalized for allowing such mistakes to leave the facility, creating a culture where errors

This is one of the most outrageous claims in the book, yet it has gone unnoticed as no reviews have pointed it out. Mint employees were never punished for errors leaving the facility. Mistakes escaped the mint simply because no one noticed the error. There's no evidence the mint ever worried about error coins, nor any record of error coin mintages. It was part of minting coins. If there was a report on an issue, they would make a correction to the dies. Error coins only gained significance in the collecting community when grading services started recognizing them in 1999.

The book incorrectly claims that double denominations are planchet errors. In fact, these errors occur when the mint mistakenly uses dies intended for two different denominations.

pieces or curiosities. The 1913 Liberty Head nickel, for instance, was initially dismissed by many as a mere oddity or possibly even a counterfeit, rather than the multi-million dollar rarity it's now known to be.

This story is made up, as the release of this nickel was never labeled counterfeit or an oddity. Due to the rarity of the coin, some original coins might have been suspected of being counterfeit but were later confirmed as authentic.

As you hunt for these striking errors, remember that authenticity is key. Some, like off-centers or broadstrikes, can be easily faked by manipulating normal coins. Familiarize

It's impossible to authentically fabricate an off-center coin from one already struck, and expanding a coin into a broadstruck version without leaving tooling marks is challenging. An experienced author would instead highlight what to look for in counterfeit coins, such as Chinese replicas.

It is absurd to claim that error coin dealers arose in the 1970s because specialized dealers for error coins didn't exist until numismatists like Bill Fivaz and J.T. Stanton began recognizing and cataloging them in the 1970s. The FS grading system, later used by PCGS, was developed by these two experts.

Chapter Two – You Are Being Scammed

To clarify, examine the scams in Steele's book, available for free. It's baffling that anyone would buy this book and give it five stars. People are ranking it number one without any logical justification. This would be acceptable if not for the inaccurate information it contains.

How this book will not make you an expert
Steele's work lacks originality and won't make you an expert. Everything in it can be found in other authors' works, which provide accurate information about coins. Presenting Steele's material to a coin dealer will likely lead to disputes over the rarities and coins discussed in his book.

Untruth 1: It's striking to observe the audacity of self-published authors copyrighting material already under copyright, as they've plagiarized it from unknown sources. If you want the photos from these books, just take them, they did.

Steele's Introduction

Untruth 2: The introduction makes the claim that Owen Steele is a renowned numismatist and best-selling author. After reading this book, it's clear that Owen Steele is not a renowned numismatist or bestselling author on American coinage. He's a con artist. No true expert randomly pulls coins from the internet, compiles them into a book, and misidentifies many of them.

> Error coins are the mavericks of numismatics, those delightful aberrations that slipped through the US Mint's quality control, each telling a unique story of its creation. From the subtle nuances of doubled dies to the striking anomalies of off-center strikes, these numismatic treasures offer a window into the minting process and a chance to own a piece of history gone awry. 4

This passage seems AI-generated, crafted as a well-structured narrative but devoid of real substance. Deeper into the book, the writing quality noticeably declines.

Untruth 3: The claim is made that a person will develop the skills for making four figures. Nothing in Steele's book will guide anyone to turn pocket-change Lincoln cents into four-figure rarities. This

---

4 Steele's introduction from his book

paragraph is crafted to lure people into buying this worthless book.

After examining over 60 self-published books on Amazon, either through Kindle or by purchasing them, it's evident that two coins appear in many of these deceptive books, the 1955 doubled die and 1943 copper cents.

Untruth 4: The book states that seasoned numismatists can elevate their expertise with his book. No veteran numismatist will commend this book, as it offers nothing for them but amusement.

How this book will not make you an expert
Untruth 5: Steele makes the claim that his book will "equip you with the tools to differentiate between valuable errors and post-mint damage.[5]" Steele's mistaken claim that the 1937-D three-legged Buffalo nickel is a die break error is easily debunked. Any experienced coin collector recognizes this as false.

Untruth 6: Steele claims his book equips readers to distinguish valuable errors from man-made ones, yet he provides no examples to support this.
He suggests you'll learn to use a loupe to identify die cracks and cuds. If someone can't spot these errors with a basic magnifying glass, they might

---

[5] Owen Steele's book

consider buying this book. However, any cud adding significant value is visible without magnification.

Untruth 7: Steele's suggestion to "rifle" through Kennedy half-dollar rolls for the No "FG" variety is impractical, as these rolls are hard to obtain without purchasing them. His mention of a 1982 Lincoln cent "no-brass" error, without noting that both copper-plated zinc and copper cents were minted in 1982, reveals ignorance or lazy research. The only notable error is the 1982-D small date copper cent, which was never meant to be minted. It's clear by now that Steele's book is a scam. He fabricates a "rare" 1999 Wide AM Lincoln cent with misaligned columns, an error that doesn't exist and couldn't occur due to hub design precision.

Untruth 8: Steele claims to teach the "nuances" of preserving error coins by knowing when to encapsulate them through grading services. It's simple: encapsulation costs about $70, so if an error coin's value is less than that, it's not worth it. Many lack this knowledge, leading to thousands of low-value error coins being encapsulated and sold at auctions for less than $20, despite the $70 encasement cost.

Untruth 9: Steele promises that by the book's end, you'll master the language of die states. Instead, you'll be left demanding a "refund." He confuses die states with die cracks and never revisits the topic.

Part One
Untruth 10: Steele falsely claims that mint errors were historically ignored or destroyed. In truth, numerous error coins exist from early mintages and were not destroyed, though often overlooked in collections. Purchasing a set of Lincoln cents from the 1960s could yield RPM errors or doubled dies, many of which were discovered in older collections. These errors weren't cataloged until the 1970s by Fiaz and Stanton.

Chapter One in Steele's book
Untruth 11: Steele claims that many early error coins were destroyed by the U.S. Mint and that those reaching circulation were met with public disdain. This is inaccurate and lacks historical evidence. Misstruck coins were not considered "damaged goods" but were often set aside as novelties. The advent of third-party grading services like PCGS, NGC, and ANACS led to a surge in error coin encapsulations, as collectors sought professional authentication, not because the coins were previously shunned.

Untruth 12: Steele also falsely asserts that third-party grading services legitimized error coin collecting. In reality, error coin catalogs and classifications began emerging in the 1970s, driven by numismatic experts, not grading services.

Untruth 13: Additionally, Steele's claim that the 1955 doubled die Lincoln cent sparked widespread scrutiny of pocket change for errors is incorrect. According to Coin World, the collector and dealer base grew significantly after the 1960 launch of the magazine, fueled by excitement over the "rare" 1960 Small Date Lincoln cents. By 1964, the number of collectors and dealers had increased roughly tenfold from the mid-1950s, with Chet Krause of Numismatic News estimating at least 6,000 dealers in the U.S., many operating shops.[6]

Untruth 14: Steele further misleads by citing the U.S. Mint's release of silver dollars in the 1960s as a driver of collecting surges. This is false, as no silver dollars were released for circulation in the 1960s. Coin collecting expanded due to publications, the American Numismatic Association (ANA), and other organizations, not a silver dollar event. Steele overlooks the GSA Hoard, a cache of approximately 2.9 million Morgan silver dollars, mostly from the Carson City Mint, discovered in Treasury vaults in the early 1960s. These coins were not released until 1972, when the General Services Administration (GSA) authorized their sale through mail-bid auctions,

---

[6] Coin World

encased in special GSA holders.[7] This hoard, primarily uncirculated Carson City Morgans, was a significant numismatic event, but it occurred in the 1970s and was largely inaccessible to the average collector due to cost, contrary to Steele's narrative.

Chapter Two in Steele's book

Untruth 15: Steele asserts that die errors arise from issues during die creation or damage during minting. While not entirely wrong, his explanation is incomplete and oversimplified. Die errors also include misaligned die errors, where dies are not properly aligned, causing off-center designs on one side of the coin. Repunched mintmark (RPM) errors occur when a mintmark is punched multiple times, leaving traces of the earlier mark. Clashed die errors happen when dies strike each other without a planchet, transferring design elements between them, resulting in coins with faint outlines of opposing designs (e.g., the "Bugs Bunny" Franklin Half Dollar). Mule errors, rare and significant, result from pairing dies of different denominations, such as a nickel obverse with a cent reverse.

Untruth 16: Steele's claim that doubled die errors are the "crown jewels" of error coins is misleading. The most valuable error coins, like the 1943 bronze and 1944 steel cents, stem from wrong-

---

[7] Coin World

planchet errors, which command higher prices due to rarity and historical significance. Steele further misleads by suggesting that doubled dies are popularly believed to result from striking a planchet twice. This is false; doubled dies occur during die creation when a die receives multiple, misaligned hub impressions, causing duplicated design elements on all coins struck by that die.

Untruth 17: Steele incorrectly cites the 1944-D/S Walking Liberty half dollar as an RPM example, when it is actually an overmintmark (OMM) error, where a die originally punched with one mintmark (e.g., "S") is repurposed with another (e.g., "D"). Contrary to Steele's claim that the 1944-D/S is a "coveted rarity," it is one of many OMM errors and not particularly notable among collectors.

Untruth 18: Steele overstates the significance of die cracks and breaks, calling them a "crucial area of study." Die cracks are extremely common, appearing on billions of coins, and are minor unless significant. Die breaks are less frequent and may result in a cud if a piece of the die breaks away, leaving a blank area on the coin. Steele inaccurately describes retained cuds, which occur when a broken die fragment remains held by the collar, not when the die piece "falls away."

Untruth 19: Finally, Steele's claim that dies are routinely filed down to achieve proper relief is outdated. While filing occurred in the 19th and early 20th centuries to adjust relief or repair dies, by 1990, advancements like computer-aided design (CAD) and precision hubbing eliminated the need for manual filing. Modern dies have relief controlled during the hubbing process at the master die or hub stage, ensuring consistency without manual alterations to working dies.

Prior to 1990, mintmarks like "D" (Denver) or "S" (San Francisco) were manually punched onto working dies, primarily at the Philadelphia Mint, though occasionally at branch mints like Denver in specific cases. Mint workers used a hammer and a steel mintmark punch to imprint the letter onto the die's surface. [8] If the first punch was misaligned, too shallow, or incorrect (e.g., the wrong mintmark), a worker might re-punch the mintmark in a slightly different position or angle. This resulted in a repunched mintmark (RPM), where remnants of the initial punch remained visible on the die, appearing as an overlapping or shadowed mintmark on coins struck by that die.

Planchet Errors
Untruth 20: Steele claims planchet errors occur only before a coin is struck, but thousands of certified error coins exhibit split planchets caused

---

[8] US Mint

during the striking process, which are also classified as planchet errors.

Untruth 21: Steele suggests collectors should seek 1965, 1966, and 1967 transitional errors struck on silver planchets instead of copper-nickel clad planchets. While such errors are theoretically possible, finding 1966 or 1967 examples is extremely unlikely, bordering on impossible, creating misleading hype about their discoverability.

Untruth 22: The assertion that canceled coins are reintroduced into the minting process and restruck is unverified, as no such coins have been documented or sold at auction.

Striking Errors in US Mint Production
Untruth 23: Steele describes a brockage error in the minting process and claims a 1977-D Jefferson nickel is a well-known example. This is misleading, as no such 1977-D brockage nickels are documented in major auction records, raising questions about the validity of his example.

Environmental Damage vs. True Errors in US Coins
Untruth 24: Steele inadequately describes strike-through errors with a single sentence, stating only that a foreign object between the die and planchet creates an impression on the coin. A more

thorough explanation would have included examples of debris, such as fibers, cloth, metal particles, or extreme cases like paper clips or nails. Instead of highlighting this common error, which can often be found in pocket change, he focuses on a rare, dropped filling error and he does not even describe it correctly. Definition from error-ref.com "This error type occurs when compacted die fill ("grease") falls out of a recess in the die face and onto a planchet. The plug of hardened material is then struck into the planchet, leaving an incuse impression of whatever design element the plug had molded itself to. Letters ("dropped letters") and numbers ("dropped numbers") are the most common elements duplicated in this fashion. If the plug remains next to the same die it fell out of, and if it doesn't flip over, the dropped letter/number is oriented the same way as its normal raised counterpart. If, however, the filling falls against the opposite die or flips over, the impression is mirror-image. Most dropped fillings are normally oriented.[9]"

Untruth 25: Steele refers to the "Blakesley effect" as a valid term for clipped planchet errors but misinterprets it, claiming it involves "design elements near the clip being distorted due to metal flow during striking." This is incorrect, and the

---

[9] Error-ref.com

term is outdated in modern numismatics. The correct definition is: A weak or incomplete rim strike, often with a faint or "shadow" design on the rim opposite the clipped or misaligned area, caused by the planchet tilting or shifting, reducing die contact on one side.

Chapter 4 – Essential Tools for US Error Coin Identification

Untruth 26: Steele incorrectly states that a genuine 1942 copper cent measures 19.05mm, while a 1943 steel cent measures 19.00mm. Both coins share the same diameter of 19.05mm.

Untruth 27: Steele advises collectors to invest in gauge pins or pin gauges to measure die cracks or holes in coins, which is impractical and unnecessary. Die cracks do not increase a coin's value based on their size, and holes typically reduce a coin's value. Furthermore, suggesting calipers to identify doubled die coins is unrealistic and misleading.

Chapter 5 - Step by Step Instructions for Identifying Error Coins in Circulation

Criticism: The primary flaw in this chapter is the lack of step-by-step guidance for identifying error coins in circulation. Discussing tools like calipers, scales, and magnifying glasses does not constitute instructions; these are merely devices, not a methodical approach to error coin identification.

Untruth 28: Steele suggests using a digital scale and caliper to identify a 1943 copper cent, but this is misleading. The copper color of a 1943 Lincoln cent is the initial indicator. If the coin doesn't weigh approximately 3.11 grams, it may be counterfeit. The only definitive way to confirm authenticity is through professional grading by PCGS, NGC, or ANACS.

Untruth 29: Steele's claim that a digital microscope is necessary to detect a 1969-S doubled die Lincoln cent is incorrect. A 10x loupe is sufficient to reveal all necessary details, and collectors with sharp vision may not require any tools.

Untruth 30: Steele's assertion that a stereo microscope is needed to identify error coins is unnecessary. For instance, the 2019 doubled die Lincoln cent requires careful study with a 10x loupe to confirm, as it's a subtle doubled die, but a stereo microscope is not essential. The US Error Coin Guide by Stan McDonald is a valuable resource, detailing eight types of doubled dies to aid in detecting DDOs.

Untruth 31: Steele's claim that collectors are likely to find off-center coins in circulation is misleading. He suggests the Mint catches major off-center errors but releases coins with 5-10% off-center strikes into circulation. The Mint ships coins in bags to Federal Reserve Banks, which distribute them to major banks. Off-center coins that don't fit standard coin rolls are typically rejected during the bank's rolling process, making it highly unlikely for any off-center coins to reach circulation through commercial bank distribution.

Common Errors Found in US Pocket Change
There is nothing in this section that should not be known. It is just a word salad.

Chapter 10: Legendary US Die Errors
Untruth 32: The book's structure is unprofessional, skipping from Chapter 5 to Chapter 10, suggesting Steele is not a credible author.

The Facts: Steele correctly notes that the 1937-D three-legged Buffalo nickel resulted from a mint worker attempting to remove a die clash. However, this contradicts his earlier claim that it was caused by a die break error. Such conflicting explanations suggest one version was fabricated, likely with the accurate account sourced from the internet.

Additionally, Chapter 10's list of error coins is a disjointed collection of rare errors that collectors are unlikely to encounter, with no clear rationale for their selection. Why focus on these five when more recognized error coins exist?

1937-D Three-Legged Buffalo Nickel
1955 Doubled Die Lincoln Cent
1982 No "FG" Kennedy Half Dollar
2004-D Wisconsin Extra Leaf Quarter
2009 District of Columbia Doubled Soapbox Quarter

Chapter 11: Remarkable US Planchet Errors
1943 Copper Cent
1944 Steel Cent
1965 Silver Dime (Struck on Silver Planchet)
1982 No Brass Lincoln Cent
Untruth 34: Steele states: "The No Brass Lincoln Cent error occurred when a few planchets composed entirely of zinc, without the copper plating, made their way through the minting process." This is not a rare coin since many example of copper-zinc Lincoln cents missing the copper coating are available.
2000-P Sacagawea Dollar/Washington Quarter Mule

Untruth 35: Choosing just five so-called "remarkable" error coins, including one that isn't a true rarity, suggests this book was authored by a profit-driven writer lacking genuine collecting expertise.

Chapter 12: Exceptional US Striking Errors 1999-2000 Wide AM Lincoln Cents

Untruth 36: The 1999 and 2000 wide Lincoln cents are not striking errors but varieties resulting from the accidental use of proof dies.

Untruth 37: Steele claims the 2000-P Wide AM is rare, but this variety is common, frequently found in circulation, with examples selling for under $5. Omitting the 1998 and 1988 Wide AM varieties further reveals a lack of coin collecting expertise. He also fails to mention the close AM varieties.

"**Lincoln Cents - Wide AM**
1988 wide AM, Flared FG (MS63, $240) (MS66, $575)
1988-D wide AM (MS63, $130)
1998 wide AM (MS65, $50-$75) (MS66, $60-$120) (MS67, $240-$940)
1999 wide AM (MS62, $80) (MS63, $120-$130) (MS64, $100-$210) (MS65, $140-$480) (MS66, $175-$470) (MS67, $660-$1,260) (MS68, $3,960)
2000 wide AM (MS66, $20-$95) (MS67, $130-$185)."[10]

"**Lincoln Cents - Close AM**
1992 (MS61, $1,705) (MS62, $4,800) (MS64, $8,810-$22,800) (MS67, $25,850)
1992-D (AU55, $960-$2,230) (AU58, $960-$5,640) (MS62, $1,140-$3,055) (MS63, $1,680-$4,260) (MS64,

---

[10] From the US Error Coin Guide 2025 by Stan McDonald

$2,280-$5,140) (MS65, $3,120-$8,400) (MS66, $8,415-$12,000)[11]"

2007-2008 Presidential Dollars with Missing Edge Lettering

Untruth 38: Steele's emphasis on 2007 and 2008 Presidential dollars missing edge lettering reveals a limited understanding of the full scope of minting errors.

Presidential Dollars - Missing Letter Edge

2007-P George Washington, missing edge lettering (MS64, $75)

2007-P John Adams, missing edge lettering (MS65, $60-$265)

2008-P James Monroe, missing edge lettering (MS68, $315)

2008-P Martin Van Buren, missing edge lettering (MS65, $95-$100) (MS66, $145) (MS67, $90-$100)

2008-P William Harrison, missing edge lettering (MS66, $100)

2010-P Millard Fillmore, missing edge lettering (MS66, $50)

Off-Center Strikes: From Minor to Major in US Coins
1955 "Bugs Bunny" Franklin Half Dollar
1974-D Aluminum Lincoln Cent

Untruth 39: Selecting a few coins and deeming them exceptional, when many other notable

---

[11] From the US Error Coin Guide 2025 by Stan McDonald

examples exist, highlights a lack of expertise in coin collecting.

Chapter 13: Modern US Errors (21st Century) 2009-2021 Lincoln Cent Errors

Misrepresentation: By this chapter, the book significantly declines, featuring filler coins with no purpose beyond padding pages. The selections and writing style become simplistic and juvenile.

The "Extra Finger" variety on the Log Splitter reverse
Doubled Die Obverses (DDOs) and Doubled Die Reverses (DDRs) across all four designs, with the Formative Years (Log Splitter) DDR being particularly sought after.
Various off-center strikes, with some dramatic examples missing large portions of the design.
The 2010 "Spaghetti Head" Lincoln
Multiple years featuring "Skinny Lincoln" varieties.
The 2014 D/D RPM
The 2017-P "Dropped Letter" variety

Untruth 40: There is no definitive evidence that confirms a 2010 Lincoln cent variety or error officially named "Spaghetti Head." This term is not recognized in standard numismatic catalogs like CONECA, Wexler's doubleddie.com, or the Cherrypickers' Guide.

Untruth 41: There is no widely recognized Lincoln cent variety officially termed "Skinny Lincoln" in numismatic references.

Untruth 42: No 2014 D/D RPM is listed in major numismatic references like CONECA's RPM Book, Wexler's listings, or the Cherrypickers' Guide.

Untruth:43 There is no record for a 2017-P Lincoln cent with a dropped letter and even if there were, this is not a valuable coin.

America the Beautiful Quarter Errors

2004-D Wisconsin Extra Leaf quarters

2015-P Bombay Hook (Delaware) Doubled Die Reverse.

The 2017-P Frederick Douglass (Washington D.C.) quarter offers another intriguing error: the "Shattered Die" variety.

2018-P Apostle Islands (Wisconsin) quarter with the "Extra Tree" variety.

2016-D Shawnee (Illinois) quarter struck 50% off-center.

The 2011-P Glacier (Montana) quarter with a large die cud

Untruth: 44 The section in America the Beautiful errors seems like a superficial internet search used to pad the book. By this point, the content unravels, rendering the book little more than kindling for a fireplace.

Coins like Bombay Hook are only recognized in Wexler's catalog and are of no significance. No, a specific "Shattered Die" variety for the 2017-P Frederick Douglass National Historic Site Quarter is not documented in major numismatic references (CONECA, Wexler, PCGS, NGC, or Cherrypickers' Guide).

No, an "Extra Tree" variety for the 2018-P Apostle Islands National Lakeshore Quarter is not recognized in standard references. The reverse depicts a sea cave with kayakers, not a prominent tree, making an "extra tree" unlikely as a design element

American Innovation Dollar Errors
1. Missing edge lettering:
2. Doubled edge lettering:
3. Weak or partial edge lettering:
1. Off-center strikes:
2. Broadstrikes:
3. Double strikes:
4. Die cracks and cuds;
5. Doubled dies:

The book's focus on off-center strikes, broadstrikes, double strikes, die cracks, and doubled dies, while omitting other common error types, reveals its shortcomings and suggests it was written by a novice.

2007 Washington Presidential Dollar with Smooth Edge
2009 Ultra High Relief Double Eagle
Including a 2007 Washington Presidential Dollar and a 2009 double eagle in the book, when many other coins could have been chosen, shows a clear lack of expertise and an attempt to merely fill pages.

Chapter Three - Narratives, Catchy Words and Phrases

Narratives

Narratives hook readers into buying books. Amazon's "read sample" feature previews a snippet, but it's often polished and misrepresents the book's disorganized, poorly written content. Per Merriam-Webster, a narrative is a story or account, often framing events to push a viewpoint. Most error coin guides lean on sales-driven narratives and catchy phrases to lure buyers, unlike credible guides that simply list content without gimmicks.

Analyzing purchased books revealed frequent use of words like "expert," "discover," "embark," "essential," and "delve" to narrate and entice.

Catchy Narratives

Examples absent from expert-authored guides include:

- "A vast sea of online info overwhelms collectors—our handbook saves the day."
- "Build your collection like a pro."
- "Own history and boost your finances."
- "Embark on your collecting adventure."

Catchy Words
Common buzzwords include budding, captivating, connoisseurs, crucial, decipher, delicate, demystifies, dive, elusive, embark, empower, essential, exciting, exhilarating, expert, fascinating, and journey.

Delve
"Delve" dominates descriptions:

- "A deep delve into coin history and artistry."
- "Delve into coin collecting's world."
- "We delve into annealing processes…"
- "Delve into nickels, dimes…"
- "Delve into planchet and die errors…"

Financial Profit Fallacy
Books promising wealth from coin collecting lack credibility. Pocket change won't make you rich, and their advice is shaky. Most coins don't appreciate enough for profit—high-end coins (valued in thousands) might, but fees often erode gains.

Chapter Four – Book Cover, Title, Fonts, Summaries and Sample Reads

Book Cover

Tracking books under 100,000 BSR shows no edge for professional covers. Many tout bonuses, "several books in one," or photo counts (e.g., "350 photos," though one had just 132). As of February 6, 2025, the top 10 included three professional designs, plus:

- One with 6 bonuses
- One with 120 photos
- One with 100 photos
- One with 350 photos (132 actual)
  C-2

As of May 2025, the top ten books with BSR's under 100,000 reveal a change in designs. One major change is adding an American flag and a "color" circle which is a ploy by those who are not writing books in the USA. The book covers listing the number of photos in the book have dropped off the BSR threshold. Book one is professional, and it is not included in the analysis.

A few observations:
- All books feature photos from Heritage Auctions or NGC, used without permission.
- Three books mark color with a circle.

- Two books display American flags, though this design is becoming more common.
- Nine books have historical British names. Most of the error coin guides on Amazon do have British names. I hypothesize that 95% of these books are authored by foreign entities using historical English names sourced from the internet.

Poor covers tank sales: a U.S. error guide with a faded Chinese lantern and "Fortune" as the author sits at 2.2M BSR (0–1 sales/month). Others with odd coin images rank at 3.4M or 4M, or lack placement entirely, suggesting cover-driven rejection.

Book Titles
Successful titles get copied or tweaked—a 2024 trend fueling the error coin book boom. Amazon doesn't protect titles, enabling duplicates. As of March 10, 2025, 182 guides exist, many mimicking established names.

The book failure rate for 2025 is 94% based on estimated sales equating to a BSR under 35,000.

Update March 18, 2025: The newest scheme by dishonest writers is to state "latest edition" when there were no previous issues.

Categories
All coin books on amazon can be categorized by content.

- Beginner Books
- Beginner Error Coin Books
- Beginner with World Coins
- Coin Guides
- Error Coin Guides
- Error Coin Searching Guides
- Error Coin Guides (Varieties)
- Pocket Change Guides
- World Coins
- World Error Coins

Font Styles
Most error coin covers share similar fonts, except one unranked book with cosmetic flaws.

Book Cover Colors
As of May 2025, the newly release books feature black, gold, silver, and white on the covers but success isn't tied to them—top 100,000 books vary.

Publication Year & Repeat Authors:
Few authors update annually due to low profits, or they are removed from Amazon for plagiarism.

Exceptions: Stan McDonald (yearly since 2010), Sam Sommer (since 2018), and Ken Potter/Brian Allen (2021 book in top 10). In 2024, 26 author-named books went out of print; by March 10, 2025, 40 did—some likely for infringement.

Book Summary and Sample Read
Summaries split into informational (content-focused) and enticements (wealth/expertise promises). Popular words: "delve," "discover," "expert," plus crafted, dive, elevate, embark, empower, exclusive, and explore. There is no proof that ties summaries to top 100 status.

Professional Writing Companies
Promotion sites claim lower BSR boosts sales. Scribe Media offers writing guidance, pushing professional covers and graphics. (Note: This book cites Scribe as an example, not an endorsement.)

Chapter Five – Categories, Key Words and Promoting

Categories

Amazon offers three category slots per book. Most error guides use **Best Sellers in Antiques & Collectibles Encyclopedias**. Some have obscure categories, but it's unclear if any of the categories help since most people use the Amazon search box and type in key words like "error coin guides" instead of searching by category. The top 100 books are listed in each category on Amazon.

As of May 21, 2025, "Strike It Rich" leads as the top book on error coins, authored by professionals. Owen Steele's book, ranked second in the study, faces credibility concerns due to inaccuracies and misleading claims, placing seventh in Amazon's category ranking. A top 100 ranking doesn't ensure strong sales, as books with a BSR above 35,000 generally yield low profits.

The "Best Sellers in Antiques & Collectibles Encyclopedias" category may influence sales for books in the top 100, but there's no evidence that buyers use this category to find error coin books, relying instead on keyword searches. The chart below displays the author's names and their rankings in the top 100 books for the category. Some of these books are not error coin guides but instead cover world coins or general coin topics.

Key Words
Keywords drive searches on Amazon's creation site. Optimal terms match buyer intent, yet even top keywords (e.g., "error coin guide") don't guarantee visibility. The test book results confirm that keywords will not always generate specific results.

Promoting Books
Scribe suggests leveraging influences and paid promotion. Later in this book it is revealed that influencers are not always truthful.

Scribe Media recommends using a book promotion site and paying for the service. They also make some other recommendations using email accounts and promotional sites. It is not possible to acquire information to understand the impact on the sales ranking without establishing an account with Scribe Media, which is not in the interest of this book.

A search of the internet for promotional activities by third parties for the top ten books in this study with BSR 's under 100,000 reveals no connection.

Chapter Six – Best Seller, Category Rankings, Price and Profit

Amazon Book Rankings

Amazon's algorithm updates hourly. The test book moved from #120 to #118 within hours, confirming this.

Amazon explains: "Best Seller and Category Ranks are based on customer activity of your book relative to the activity of other books. Books can be ranked in up to three best seller category lists, regardless of how many categories the book may feature within. Your book's customer activity influences which three categories the book can be ranked in and will appear on the book's detail page. For example, a book ranking #1 in Mystery & Thrillers is the book with the most activity in Amazon's Mystery & Thrillers category. A book's Best Sellers Rank in each category shows under the Product Details section on the book's detail page. Activities that may not be an accurate reflection of customer demand, such as canceled orders, are not counted toward sales rank.

Rankings are updated hourly but may take 24–48 hours to appear. Rankings reflect recent and historical activity, with recent activity weighed more heavily. Rankings are relative, so your sales rank can change even when your book's level of activity stays the same. For example, even if your book's level of activity stays the same, your rank may improve if other books see a decrease in activity, or your rank may drop if other books see an increase in activity.

When we calculate Best Sellers Rank, we consider the entire history of a book's activity. Monitoring your book's Amazon sales rank may be helpful in gaining general insight into the effectiveness of your marketing campaigns and other initiatives to drive book activity, but it is not an accurate way to track your book's activity or compare its activity in relation to books in other categories.

The ranking for books with consistent activity histories that have been available on Amazon for a long time may fluctuate less than the ranking of new books, or books whose histories aren't as stable. One sale of a very popular book may not influence its rank much at all, but one sale of a lower volume book may significantly improve that book's rank.[12]"

---

[12] Amazon help

Amazon Best Seller Ranking by Category

Amazon provides three ways to review a book's ranking:

- Explore the top 100 best-selling books overall (coin guides are typically absent).
- Review the top 100 in a specific category through category rankings.
- Enter keywords related to the book in the Amazon search box.

Typically, an Amazon Best Seller Rank (BSR) under 100,000 corresponds to a top 100 spot in its chosen category. Most error coin guides use "Antique & Collectibles Encyclopedias" as the major category.

Authors can assign up to three sales categories per book. Amazon displays the overall top 100 in See Top 100 in Books. Below is an example with two categories selected.

Best Sellers Rank: #292,762 in Books (See Top 100 in Books)
  #198 in Antique & Collectible Coins & Medals (Books)
  #302 in Antiques & Collectibles Encyclopedias
Customer Reviews: 4.4 ★★★★☆ ∨   14 ratings

Some believe they can boost sales by using irrelevant categories for their books, hoping for an advantage. A US coin error guide is unrelated to foreign coins or coin folders.

Best Sellers Rank: #59,794 in Books (See Top 100 in Books)

    #7 in World Coins Collecting

    #23 in Collectible Coin Folders

    #42 in Antiques & Collectibles Encyclopedias

Most error coin books are categorized under Antiques & Collectibles Encyclopedias, where the top 100 can be viewed by exploring that category

Amazon doesn't offer "coin collecting" as a distinct category—searches in Crafts, Hobbies & Home or "all categories" via the search bar yield no coin guides.

Price

Most Amazon coin books are priced from $14.97 to $16.99, with sellers aligning prices based on competitors. A 115-page book priced at $14.99 yields $6.70 profit per sale. Selling 2.7 copies daily (approximately 90,000 BSR) generates about

$218 monthly, insufficient for most authors to continue writing.

Chapter Seven – Buyer Reviews and Ratings

Review Rating

Customer Reviews: 4.2 ★★★★☆ ∨   17 ratings

Customers assign books a rating of 1 to 5 stars. Uninformed buyers, unaware of inaccurate error coin listings and deceptive claims, frequently award these books five-star reviews. Conversely, credible one-star reviews point out specific inaccuracies or misleading statements, offering valuable insights, though most lack detail (e.g., "I didn't like it") and thus carry limited weight.

There's no clear explanation for why one book receives more reviews than another when both are released concurrently. For example, Owen Steele's book, released in November 2024, has 381 reviews, while Oson Kane's book, also released in November 2024, has 133 reviews. Both books meet the 100,000 BSR threshold, but Kane's book is declining in rank. There is no correlation between a book's number of reviews and its BSR number.

In May 2025, the average review rating for books with a BSR under 100,000 is 4.6 out of 5.0. Some books maintain a 4.0 or higher rating artificially, as a drop to 3.9 often prompts a next-day surge of five-star reviews. Amazon disregards requests to investigate these sudden spikes in 5.0-star reviews. Multiple books by Jason Whitmore receive 5-star reviews from the same individuals across all four titles.

Jason Whitmore 9798306678801	Jason Whitmore 9798306564838	Jason Whitmore 9798306677958	Jason Whitmore 9798306679440
Twitty	Twitty	Twitty	Twitty
Amy K.	Mayora-Tridento		
Paul Streett			
James West	James West	James West	James West
Zack			
Noah	Noah	Noah	Noah
Starship	Starship	Starship	Starship
Corky	Corky	Corky	Corky
Jellybean	Jellybean	Jellybean	Jellybean
Lindell Long	Lindell Long	Lindell Long	Lindell Long
Guga	Guga	Guga	Guga
Shaikh R Hafees			Shaikh R Hafees
Joyoart85	Joyoart85	Joyoart85	Joyoart85
J. Mielke	J. Mielke	J. Mielke	J. Mielke
V.E.	Teresa Rutrough		
	Serendipity	Serendipity	Serendipity
		Zack Clemons	
		Hanna	

The chart below tracks reviews for Lucas Ford and aliases Nick Ford, Error Collector, Gary N. Peters, Lincoln Mollett. The alias were confirmed using thirty of the same photos taken from Heritage Auctions. As of March 10, 2025, seven books by Lucas Ford and one by Nick Ford were removed for photo infringements. As of May 2025, Error Collector and Mollett have been removed from Amazon, but Peters, & Ford, and remain unscathed.

It's unlikely that the same 12 individuals are coincidentally purchasing and reviewing Lucas

Ford's books. More likely, these reviewers have ties to the author and are used to boost ratings. Below is a chart of reviewers for the now-defunct Lucas Ford books.

Name	Books Purchased
Josephine E king	12
John F. Rowan jr	7
VIC	6
Collins	5
Smylla	5
Amazon Customer	4
Amazon Customer1	4
Loveth mark	4
Baxter P	3
Benjamin Stevens	3
Fati Teslim	3
Robert Nelson jnr	3

Mathematical Impact on Ratings

Fewer reviews amplify the impact of new ones on a book's rating. For example, two five-star and two two-star reviews average 3.5; adding two one-star reviews drops it to 3.0.

Four ratings

Stars	Count	Points	Total Count	Rating
5	2	10		
2	2	4		
		14	4	3.5

Six Ratings

Stars	Count	Points	Total Count	Rating
5	2	10		
2	4	8		
		18	6	3.0

A book with 105 reviews and a 4.8-star rating would need 20 additional one-star reviews, with no recent reviews of other ratings, to reduce its average to 4.3. An additional 15 one-star reviews would be required to lower it to 4.0.

Stars	Count	Points	Total Count	Ratings
5	100	500		
1	5	5		
		505	105	4.8

Stars	Count	Points	Total Count	Ratings
5	100	500		
1	20	20		
		520	120	4.3

Stars	Count	Points	Total Count	Ratings
5	100	500		
1	35	35		
		535	135	4.0

Types of ratings

There are three types of ratings: one without a review, another with an opinion but no examples, and a third backed by credible examples. Only ratings with detailed examples explaining why a book is exceptional or flawed should matter to potential buyers. After over a year of research, it's clear that reviews don't significantly affect book sales, as many buyers seem to ignore them, even when negative reviews highlight clear inaccuracies. However, a low rating below 3.5 may influence sales, as many people quickly check this number.

While many books with BSRs in the millions boast high ratings of 4.0 to 5.0, all books rated below 3.5 have BSRs exceeding 500,000, signaling no sales.

Chapter Eight – Author Name, Bios, Author Photo, Foreign Authors, Editorials, and Expertise

Author Name

Certain authors opt for pen names when authoring books, and there's nothing inherently shady about it. But some exploit it to flood the market, pumping out more of the same or slightly tweaked titles under different aliases.

Some authors pick book titles or pseudonyms that are tough to decipher and might even hurt sales. Take these author name standouts: Henry Mintworth, Fortune Riley, Liberty Chase, Error Collector, Alex Coinman, Mark Alloy, and Benjamin Collector. As of February 12, 2025, Benjamin Collector's work is out of print. Error Collector's book is no longer available as of May 2025.

The pseudonym 'Error Collector' is tied to someone flooding the market, likely chosen as a crafty way to snag clicks on Amazon when people search for 'error collector.' It does the trick by pulling in views, but it also drags up a slew of other errors in coin books in the results. There are two books remaining from this author which have high BSR's and are insignificant.

These are some names that appear suspicious
Fortune Riley (has a Chinese lantern on the book cover)

Alex **Coinman** (only 12 people in the US have this name

Henry **Mintworth** (called out this person for lying about finding 1969-S DDO in his attic, then he removed his claims)

John Adams (sounds too much like a former president.

Eathan **Craftwell** (no ethic origin)

Jason Alexander (Seinfield)

Error **Collector** (200 stolen photos)

Liberty Chase (fake bio)

Mark **Alloy** (fake bio)

Miles Harding (fake bio)

Peter Simon (Peter and Simon)

Collector's Gateway (questionable source)

Some names might be genuine, but they seem dubious. Certain con artists likely find it amusing to invent such names.

Foreign Authors
Research in May 2025 revealed that 90% of self-published books on error coins feature last names of English origin. This aligns with numerous fabricated biographies, likely authored by individuals in India or other countries using British-style English for writing or translation. The

remaining 10% of names are German or untraceable, such as "Error Collector."

Many of these books exhibit grammar and word choices typical of European writers, while others lack credible numismatic expertise. Each book I reviewed starts with a polished writing style but deteriorates, suggesting AI-generated content.

Some self-published books, particularly those written by foreign authors, use British names for authors or characters to appeal to English-speaking markets or mask their origins. This practice can be part of dishonest self-publishing tactics, especially when combined with AI-generated content or plagiarized elements, with concerns about AI author photos and plagiarized photos.

Context and Concerns: Foreign authors may adopt British pseudonyms to gain credibility or blend into markets like the UK or US, where British names might seem more familiar or authoritative. For example, a numismatics book might be authored by someone claiming to be "James Worthington" but written by a non-native English speaker using AI tools. This can mislead readers, especially if the writing quality deteriorates (as you observed from bio to later chapters) or if the author's photo is AI-generated, showing unnatural symmetry. Such tactics erode trust and can involve plagiarism, like using stock or stolen images for covers or profiles.

Author Photos
While many author photos appear suspicious, some can be confirmed as sourced from the internet or AI-generated. AI-created images appear overly perfect and are identified as fake when analyzed by AI detection tools.

AI-Generated Author Photos
The use of AI-generated images, including author photos, is increasingly common in self-publishing. These photos can appear highly realistic but are often identifiable by unnatural symmetry or artifacts, as seen in the case of Scott Tyler below. Tools like Originality.ai can detect such content, but many authors use these images to create a professional appearance without disclosing their artificial nature, raising ethical concerns about misrepresentation. Because Amazon has low barriers to self-publishing, it enables the creation of books using AI, stolen photos, and plagiarism.

Scott Tyler - ISBN 9798312275766
A self-published book by Scott Tyler claiming expertise in numismatics. The author's photo seemed suspicious, and after analysis, it was confirmed to be 99% AI-generated due to its symmetrical perfection. While reading, I noticed a

decline in writing quality from the bio to the preface and into the later sections of the book.

His bio reads, "Scott Tyler is a 40-year-old American coin enthusiast and expert, with over two decades of experience in numismatics. As a passionate collector and historian, Scott has dedicated his career to studying U.S. error coins, their value, and their impact on the coin-collecting community. His extensive knowledge of rare minting mistakes, combined with a keen eye for detail, makes him a trusted resource for collectors at all levels. Through this book, Scott aims to share his expertise, offering readers a comprehensive guide to discovering, identifying, and profiting from the most valuable U.S. error coins." All of this becomes questionable when the author photo is fake.

Internet Copied Author Photographs
Grant Whitlow ISNBN 9798281366915

This photograph appears to be from the 1940s.
"He's shared his insights as a guest speaker at
collector forums and through numerous
contributions to trade journals." Really? There are
no contributions from this supposed author with
any numismatic publications. This person never
gave any speeches about coins.

Author Editorials
The inclusion or exclusion of editorials in a book
appears to have little impact. Amazon's policy
permits authors to include editorials, though many
are merely fabricated fluff. While some
exaggerated claims should raise suspicion, even
the most egregious ones don't prevent a book from
achieving a 100,000 BSR.

Certain authors falsely attribute numismatic titles
to their books or rely on fabricated coin

organizations for editorial reviews. Authors who reference numismatic groups without approval risk having their work removed. For example, in 2024, a book was withdrawn after the author inaccurately claimed a coin magazine had provided an editorial review. Unbeknownst to the author, I had contributed articles to that magazine.

Given that editorials lack credibility, Amazon ought to either overhaul the system or scrap the feature entirely.

Author Biographies

Amazon's lenient policies permit authors to publish biographies with misleading claims. Many assert numismatic expertise and affiliations with prominent organizations, but checks with these groups confirm no credibility. Some outlandish claims include delivering speeches or offering training expertise. Reading these books reveals substantial evidence contradicting the biographies' assertions.

Author Biographies & Expertise

Amazon's lack of guidelines for author biographies and photos allows individuals to create exaggerated or fabricated profiles for nonexistent authors. The most egregious cases involve claims of the author being a renowned numismatic expert or a widely respected figure. Verifying such claims is straightforward by consulting reputable numismatic organizations.

A look at 42 books revealed that every single one—100%—contains inaccurate info and misleading claims. The biographies are bogus, and many author photos are clearly photoshopped, with two matched to online sources via Google photo search.

Here is the author's biography from a book that recently hit the 100,000 BSR threshold. It was easy to identify credibility issues with this book. All the photos were sourced from NGC and other well-known numismatic sites, undermining the author's claim of expertise since none of the images are his own.

About the author

Richard Haskin is a respected numismatist based in Chicago with over two decades of experience specializing in U.S. error coins and varieties. His methodical approach to error identification has helped countless collectors make significant discoveries in circulation finds and dealer inventories.

Known for his ability to explain complex minting processes in accessible terms, Haskin has contributed to numerous numismatic publications and maintains an active presence in collector communities nationwide. His particular expertise in Lincoln cent and Jefferson nickel varieties has made him a sought-after speaker at coin shows and club meetings throughout the western United States.

When not examining coins through his trusted loupe, Haskin enjoys sharing his knowledge with the next generation of collectors through his popular educational workshops and online tutorials.

He couldn't have assisted anyone with significant discoveries, as the only findings in his book are photos taken from others' work. Undoubtedly, no one sought him to lead any workshop—unless it was on how to write a fraud book.

Look closely at this person's attire and the background in the photo.

Grok 3: "The photo depicts an older individual with gray hair and glasses, dressed in a dark suit, sitting at a desk. They are holding a magnifying glass and appear to be examining something closely, possibly writing or working on a detailed task. The setting looks like an old study or office, with a window in the background letting in soft light. On the desk, there are papers, a small scale, and other tools, suggesting a scholarly or scientific activity. The overall tone of the image has a vintage, sepia-like quality, giving it a historical feel. The photo has a vintage, sepia-toned aesthetic, and the attire, tools, and setting suggest an early 20th-century time, likely around the 1920s or 1930s.

If the photo is from 1930 and it's now 2025, the person depicted could be 95 years old.

Numerous coin guides on Amazon bill themselves as US error coin guides, yet their covers feature foreign coins, their pages list foreign coins, and they pass off common coins as rare or erroneous.

Many books claim an American author, but clues inside point to foreign origins. Terms like 'euros' and 'flan' pop up frequently in some, and their distinctly British tone is hard to miss.

Made in the USA
Columbia, SC
09 July 2025